JAMES EARL Carter

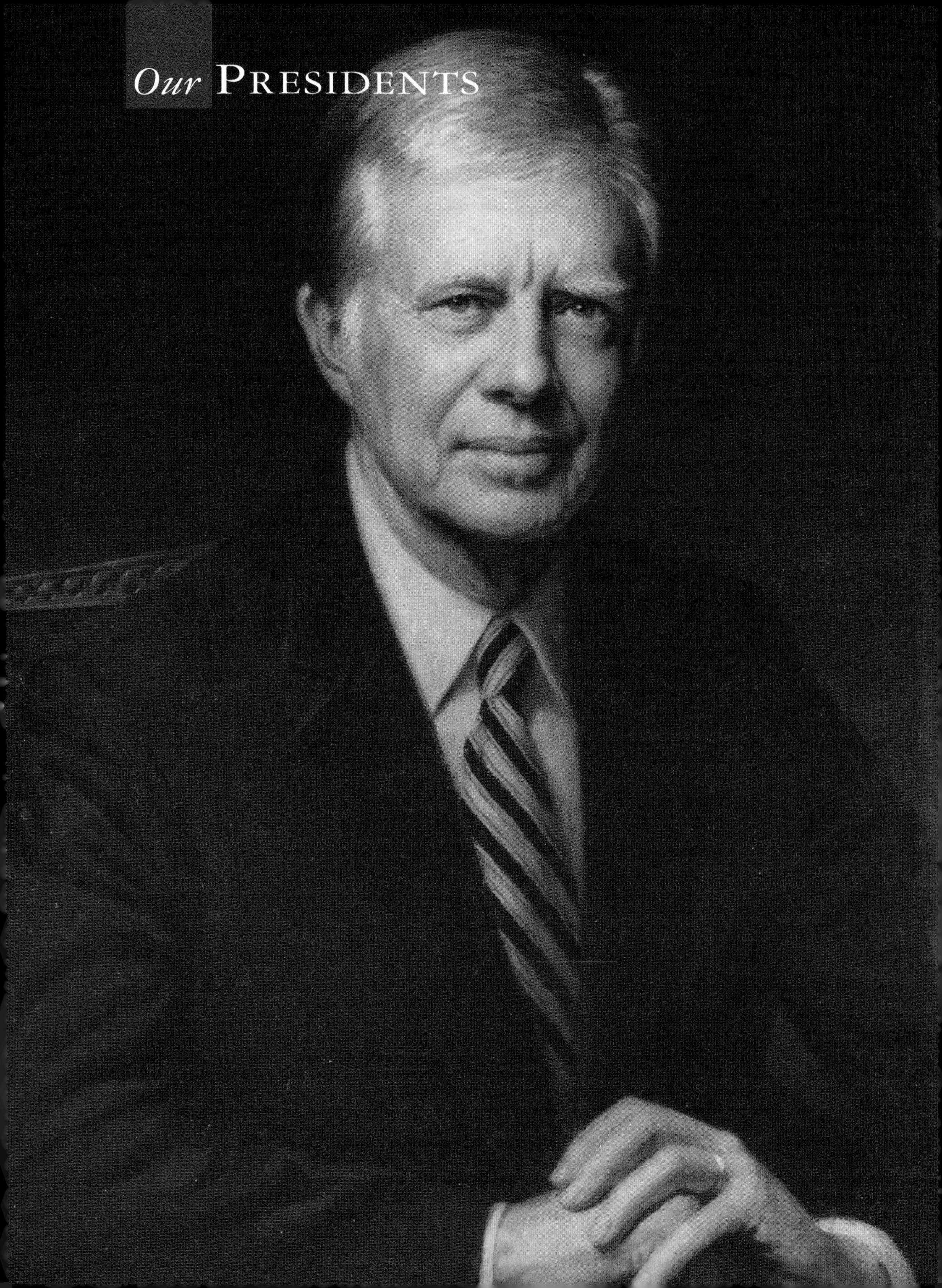

JAMES EARL *Carter*

OUR THIRTY-NINTH PRESIDENT

By Lori Hobkirk

SPIRIT
of America™

The Child's World®, Inc.
Chanhassen, Minnesota

9

JAMES EARL *Carter*

Published in the United States of America by The Child's World®, Inc.
PO Box 326 • Chanhassen, MN 55317-0326 • 800-599-READ • www.childsworld.com

Acknowledgments
The Creative Spark: Mary Francis-DeMarois, Project Director; Elizabeth Sirimarco Budd, Series Editor; Robert Court, Design and Art Direction; Janine Graham, Page Layout; Jennifer Moyers, Production

The Child's World®, Inc.: Mary Berendes, Publishing Director; Red Line Editorial, Fact Research; Cindy Klingel, Curriculum Advisor; Robert Noyed, Historical Advisor

Photos
Cover: White House Collection, courtesy White House Historical Association; all images courtesy of the Jimmy Carter Library (Atlanta, Georgia) except the following: Bettmann/Corbis: 30, 33; ©Owen Franken/Corbis: 21; ©Wally McNamee: 34; Reuters/NewMedia Inc./Corbis: 18

Registration
The Child's World®, Inc., Spirit of America™, and their associated logos are the sole property and registered trademarks of The Child's World®, Inc.

Library of Congress Cataloging-in-Publication Data
Hobkirk, Lori.
    James Earl Carter : our thirty-ninth president / by Lori Hobkirk.
        p. cm.
    Includes bibliographical references and index.
    ISBN 1-56766-873-9 (lib. bdg. : alk. paper)
    1. Carter, Jimmy, 1924—Juvenile literature. 2. Presidents—United States—Biography—
Juvenile literature. [1. Carter, Jimmy, 1924– 2. Presidents.] I. Title.
E873 .H63 2001
973.926'092—dc21

00-010948

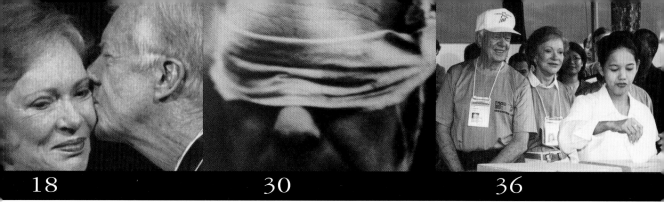

18   30   36

Contents

Chapter ONE

The Early Years

Jimmy Carter was born on October 1, 1924. He grew up in the small farm town of Plains, Georgia. From a young age, his goal was to get a good education and to attend college.

JAMES EARL CARTER, THE 39TH U.S. PRESIDENT, is best known by his nickname, "Jimmy." He first became involved in politics—the work of the government—as a young boy growing up near Plains, Georgia. His father, Earl Carter, belonged to the Democratic Party, which is one of the country's two major political parties. A political party is a group of people who share similar ideas about how to run a government.

Earl Carter was a peanut farmer, just like his son would be one day. He also owned a farm supply business. He sold tools and other items to local farmers. From his father, Jimmy learned to work hard. He also learned to take an interest in government. Earl took young Jimmy to political barbecues throughout the Georgia countryside. At these events, guests

As a young man, Jimmy Carter enjoyed sports. He played basketball at Plains High School. In this photograph of the team, he is second from left in the top row. When he attended the United States Naval Academy, he ran cross-country and played football.

spent the whole day listening to **politicians** give speeches. They exchanged political talk and enjoyed barbecued pork and chicken. Little did anyone know that Jimmy would one day become the nation's most important leader.

Jimmy's mother, Lillian, was an intelligent, open-minded person. She always listened to Jimmy's ideas. She taught him to care for the poor. She taught him about civil rights, which are the basic rights guaranteed to all American citizens. One of the most difficult issues when

7

Jimmy was growing up in the South was **segregation.** At that time, people were beginning to push for an end to this system, which used laws to keep black people and white people apart. Lillian taught Jimmy that African Americans deserved to have the same rights as white Americans.

Together, Jimmy's parents encouraged him to learn about the U.S. government and to stand up for his beliefs. Many times in his life, people challenged Jimmy's ideas about what was right and wrong. But he stuck to his beliefs.

In 1941, Jimmy graduated from Plains High School. He attended Georgia Southwestern College and later the Georgia Institute of Technology. In 1943, he was accepted to the U.S. Naval Academy in Annapolis, Maryland. Attending the academy was an honor, and Jimmy worked hard to do his best. He graduated in 1946 with a degree in **engineering.** That same year, he married Rosalynn Smith, a young woman he knew from Plains. He soon began his career in the navy, working as an engineer on submarines.

In 1953, Jimmy learned that his father was dying of cancer. By that time, Jimmy was the

Carter spent seven years in the U.S. Navy. He is pictured here, seated third from left, with his submarine crew.

chief engineer of a submarine crew. He was faced with an important decision. He, Rosalynn, and their three sons were happy living in New York, where Jimmy was working on a new submarine. But after his father died, Jimmy wanted to help his family, to support his mother, and to run the family farm and business. He longed to return to the South.

Rosalynn was unhappy with his decision, but Jimmy's mind was made up. As always, when he made a decision, nothing stopped him. Leaving the navy would change the course of his life.

Interesting Facts

▶ Carter was the first president to have graduated from the U.S. Naval Academy.

9

After their first date, Jimmy knew Rosalynn Smith was the girl for him. He went home and told his mother, "She's the girl I want to marry." This is their wedding portrait from July of 1946.

Right away, Jimmy set about improving the family's supply business. He began planting peanuts from seeds. It took several years of hard work before the businesses began to make a profit. "The entire first year I was home, our income was less than $300," he later recalled. "But we stuck it out." Jimmy

10

never had any doubt that he had made the right decision by going back home. Rosalynn helped run the businesses as well. At first, she worked only one day a week, but soon she was working full-time. In fact, she knew so much about the business that Jimmy often asked her for advice.

Meanwhile, their three sons—Jack, Chip, and Jeff—were growing up. Jimmy became a leader at his Baptist church. He also became involved with the local Lions Club. He began working with the Sumter County Board of

Jimmy never regretted his decision to move back to the family farm in Plains. With lots of hard work, he and Rosalynn made the family business a successful one.

Education and served as its head for seven years. Jimmy's main goal at the school board was to end segregation in schools. He wanted black children to attend the same schools as his sons. He wanted every child to have the same educational opportunities. This wasn't a popular view at that time in the South, but Jimmy's beliefs never wavered.

In 1962, at age 38, Jimmy decided to run for a political office. He wanted to run for the Georgia State Senate and help make laws. Running for office wasn't something Jimmy had ever imagined himself doing. But in his late 30s, he quietly considered the possibility. He wanted to become more involved in the state's education issues and serve on the senate's education committee. On an October morning in 1962, a few weeks before the election, Jimmy drove to the Sumter county seat and entered the race. Rosalynn supported his decision. In fact, she helped with the campaign whenever she had time, addressing letters, telephoning voters, and keeping records. Jimmy won the election. He and his family moved to Atlanta, the state capital. It was the beginning of a long career in politics.

In 1966, Jimmy Carter ran for governor of Georgia. He lost but then spent the next four years preparing for the next election. He traveled tirelessly around Georgia, trying to understand the state's problems. In 1970, Carter was elected the 76th governor of Georgia.

As governor, Carter made it clear that he would work to help all Georgians, especially those who most needed his assistance. "I say to you quite frankly that the time for racial discrimination is over," he said at his **inauguration.** "No poor, rural, weak, or black person should ever have to bear the additional burden of being deprived of the opportunity of an education, a job, or simple justice." His words drew attention not just from citizens in Georgia, but from people all over the nation. Together, he and Rosalynn worked to help senior citizens, children, people with mental retardation, and prisoners.

By 1972, Carter was already considering the possibility of running for president. In September of 1973, his mother, Lillian, asked him what he planned to do after leaving the governorship. Carter replied, "I'm going to run for president." She asked, "President of what?" "Momma," answered Carter, "I'm going to run for president of the United States, and I'm going to win."

Chapter TWO

At Home and Abroad

Jimmy Carter served as president from January 20, 1977, to January 20, 1981. He was the nation's 39th president.

IN 1976, THE DEMOCRATIC PARTY CHOSE Carter as its **candidate** for president. As he accepted the honor, Carter said that 1976 would be a year different from any other. "It will be a year of inspiration and hope," said Carter. "It will be a year in which we will give the government of this country back to the people of this country."

Carter also said that human rights would be an important theme of his presidency. Human rights are basic freedoms to which all people, everywhere, are entitled. Carter said it was a privilege to live in a **democracy** like the United States. Americans can help make decisions about how their government is run. In some nations, governments abuse their citizens, especially those who speak out against their leaders. Carter believed the United States should not support any government that mistreated its people. His ideas were honest and admirable. Many Americans had faith in his plans.

It was a very close election, but Carter won. Even so, when he moved into the White House the following year, many Americans

During his campaign for president, Carter traveled by train around the country to meet American citizens. He promised to never tell lies to the public and to restore trust in the U.S. government. He believed Americans had a right to know more about the activities of their leaders.

knew little about him. The United States was still recovering from the Watergate **scandal,** which had damaged Americans' trust in their leaders. The Watergate was a building where the national offices of the Democratic Party were located. Members of the Republican Party wanted information about the Democrats' plans for the next election. A group of five men broke into the offices to steal important information. By early 1973, it was clear that President Nixon and his aides had been involved in the break-in.

The Watergate scandal brought an end to President Nixon's career in politics. He was forced to leave the presidency, and Gerald Ford became president. Ford served for two years before Carter defeated him in the election of 1976.

Like other Americans, members of Congress were still angry about the Watergate scandal. They needed time to get to know and trust the new president. Its members considered Carter an outsider because he had not worked as a politician in Washington before he became president. They often made it difficult for him to reach his goals.

Even so, Carter had big plans. He wanted to protect human rights not just at home, but all around the world. He wanted to improve educational opportunities for all Americans. He wanted to work for peace in the Middle East, the region where Asia, Africa, and Europe meet. Diverse peoples and cultures live in the region. There often have been conflicts between them. Carter believed the United States could help **negotiate** a peaceful solution to some of the problems.

Another important goal for President Carter was to decrease the number of nuclear

At his inauguration, Jimmy Carter had great hope for what he might achieve as president. The nation faced many problems, but he hoped to solve them.

From the early years of their marriage, Jimmy Carter considered Rosalynn his partner. She took the job of first lady seriously. She studied the history and culture of a country before traveling. She understood her husband's position on every issue. "I am the person closest to the president of the United States," she once said, "and if I can explain his policies and let the people know of his interest and friendship, I intend to do so."

arms produced, both in the United States and in the **Soviet Union.** Nuclear arms are powerful weapons that can attack vast areas of land. They can kill and injure huge numbers of people. Carter hoped to negotiate an agreement with Soviet leaders. He wanted to reduce the risk that such weapons would ever be used.

All of these issues affected the entire world. Global problems took up most of President Carter's time. But the United States needed his attention, too. **Inflation** had been a major problem since Nixon was president. The prices of food, clothing, and other items were higher than ever before. Unemployment was high, and many people in the United States could not find jobs. Pollution and **deforestation** were destroying the nation's wilderness. Protecting the nation's environment was a necessity. Energy sources were limited, so the nation was in the midst of an energy crisis. This meant people had to cut back on their use of gasoline and electricity.

Americans doubted that Jimmy Carter could fix everything that had gone wrong in recent years. It would have been a difficult job for anybody. But Carter wanted to tackle the problems his country faced. His way of doing this was to study every part of a problem before making a decision. Some people criticized him for this habit. They said it took him too long to act.

Carter did accomplish several things during his presidency, however. He created the Depart-ment of Energy, which helped the nation use its energy sources more carefully. He also worked to protect the environment. The Alaska National Interest Lands Conservation Act protected 150 million acres of Alaskan land. Of that land, 97 million acres—an area about the size of California—was used to create new national parks and monuments. According to President Carter, signing this **bill** was one of the most satisfying acts of his presidency.

He also founded the Department of Education. Carter had always believed that educating young people should be among the nation's most important goals. He wanted more Americans to go to college. Education was a way

Fireside chats were a tradition started by another president from the Democratic Party, Franklin Roosevelt. He gave these informal talks over the radio to tell the American people what was happening in their government. President Carter carried on the tradition on television.

to ensure that the country had a bright future. But many members of Congress didn't think the president should worry about education.

It took three years to make the Department of Education a reality. Once it was founded, the department made a big difference. For one thing, it lent money to college students to help them pay for school. It also worked to improve public schools all over the nation.

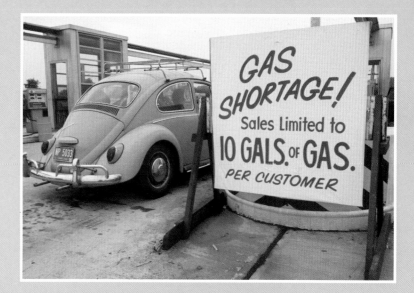

IN THE 1970s, THE ENERGY crisis was one of the most serious problems facing the nation's leaders. Americans were using more oil than any other country in the world. The world's oil supplies were running low. People began to worry that there would be no oil left one day. In addition, the price of oil kept going up. What followed was a shortage of affordable energy. People had to wait in long lines to fill their gas tanks. Some lines were a mile and a half long! Gas stations started to put limits on how much gas each person could buy. Americans had to find a way to use less energy.

Carter was determined to solve the energy crisis. He introduced an energy bill to Congress, which urged Americans to **conserve** energy. The bill also set aside money to develop new energy sources, such as solar power (energy from the sun), hydroelectric power (energy from running water), and wind power. Congress finally passed a new version of the bill 18 months after Carter introduced it.

President Carter and his staff created the Department of Energy in 1977. This wasn't an easy task, but it may have been one of his greatest achievements. Over the years, it has accomplished many things. It has worked to develop new energy sources and encouraged Americans to carpool. Thanks to the Department of Energy, houses are now built to save energy. Manufacturers make appliances that use less energy. Carter's efforts paid off. From 1977 to 1980, U.S. oil consumption dropped by 20 percent.

Chapter THREE

Treaties for Peace

International affairs took up much of President Carter's time. He enjoyed success in his dealings with other nations, but he also experienced difficulties.

PRESIDENT CARTER DEVOTED MUCH OF HIS time to problems outside the United States. Dealing with international issues was among the most challenging work of his career. Some Americans thought he spent too much time helping people in other parts of the world. They wanted him to solve problems at home first. But Carter wanted to help people wherever he could.

Soon after he became president, Carter began working on the Panama Canal **Treaty.** The Panama Canal is a waterway that opened in 1914. It was built to allow passage between the Atlantic and Pacific oceans. Before the canal was completed, ships had to travel all the way around the tip of South America. Today they can use the canal to travel through Central America.

The United States had controlled the Panama Canal since it opened in 1914, but President Carter believed that Panama should take charge of it. He and Mrs. Carter toured the canal during a visit to Central America.

The United States built and paid for the canal. Since 1914, it had taken charge of it. But the Panamanians wanted to run the canal themselves, without help from the United States. Carter agreed. He believed it was the only way to ensure friendly relations with Central America. Carter reached an agreement with Panamanian leader Omar Torrijos Herrera. A treaty would give the canal to Panama by the end of 1999. Many Americans were against the treaty. Still, President Carter was able to convince Congress to approve the treaty. The canal would belong to Panama by the end of the 20th century.

Perhaps one of Carter's most important goals was to help promote peace between the nations of Egypt and Israel. It would be a difficult task, for these peoples had been at war since Israel became a country in 1948. The creation of the nation of Israel left the Arab people of Palestine without a homeland. This angered not only the Palestinians, but other Arabs in the region as well. They believed the Israelis had wrongly taken land that had belonged to Arabs for thousands of years. There was constant warfare between Israel and neighboring Arab countries.

Over 30 years, four wars were fought between the Arabs and Israelis. Israel took control of more land that had once belonged to Arab nations. In particular, it had seized the Sinai Peninsula, a stretch of land between Israel and Egypt. The peninsula had belonged to the Egyptians, and they wanted it back. Israeli leaders refused to give it up and sent soldiers there to protect it.

Carter wanted to end the terrible warfare in the region. He hoped to forge better relations not only between Israel and Egypt, but among all nations in the Middle East.

24

Carter and Panama's leader, Omar Torrijos Herrera, signed a treaty in September of 1977. Panama promised that the canal would remain open to ships from all nations. The United States promised to give up control of the canal by the end of the 20th century. It would be 22 years after the treaty was signed before Panama actually took control of the canal.

He decided the United States should help negotiate a solution. In 1978, he organized the Camp David **Summit.**

Camp David is a small camp located in the mountains of Maryland. It is a peaceful place where the president can go for privacy and rest. Carter thought it was the perfect place to begin peace negotiations. He invited Egyptian President Anwar Sadat and Israeli Prime Minister Menachem Begin to Camp David. Carter was eager to greet the two leaders. He hoped to encourage a spirit of cooperation. He asked them to avoid arguments and angry words during their time at Camp David.

Interesting Facts

▶ Before Carter met with Prime Minister Begin and President Sadat, he wanted to learn as much about both men as he could. He studied information about their childhoods, their families, and their likes and dislikes.

President Carter thought it would take three days to reach an agreement. But it would not come that easily. Begin refused to give back Egypt's land on the Sinai Peninsula. Sadat returned to his cabin and packed his bags. Carter tried to convince Sadat to stay, but he refused. Finally, just as Sadat was about to leave for the airport, Begin agreed to return the land to Egypt.

After 13 days of long, difficult meetings, the leaders finally reached an agreement. They created the Camp David Accords, which were two separate plans. One plan outlined a peace treaty between Egypt and Israel. The other recommended ways to establish peace through-out the Middle East. The accords led to the

Carter thought the meetings at Camp David would take only three days. But he met with Prime Minister Begin (left) and President Sadat (right) for 13 days before they came to an agreement.

signing of a peace treaty. Begin, Carter, and Sadat signed the treaty on March 26, 1979. It was a first step toward ending the ancient difficulties in this troubled region.

In 1979, another part of the world demanded attention from President Carter. The Soviet Union invaded Afghanistan in late December. This was a serious problem. Americans worried that the Soviets were trying to expand their system of government, called **communism,** to other parts of the world. Communism is a system in which a country's government holds great power. Most Americans believed it was dangerous and did not want it to spread to new places.

Carter and the Soviet leader, Leonid Brezhnev, had signed the Strategic Arms Limitations Talks (SALT II) Treaty earlier that year. Now Congress had to approve it. This plan would reduce the number of nuclear arms that each nation produced. As an engineer, Carter had studied nuclear science. He knew these weapons could cause terrible destruction. He hoped SALT II would reduce this risk. But the Soviet invasion of Afghanistan threatened the SALT II Treaty.

Interesting Facts

▶ Four years after Americans boycotted the Olympic Games, the Soviet Union refused to attend the 1984 Olympics in Los Angeles. Few other nations dropped out of the Olympics that year, however. Only 81 nations had competed in Moscow, but 140 went to Los Angeles. In fact, China returned to the Olympics in 1984. Its athletes had not attended the games for 32 years.

After the invasion, Carter knew he had to show the Soviets that the United States did not approve of their actions. He asked Congress to postpone its decision about the SALT II Treaty. Then he called for a grain **embargo.** The Soviets depended on the United States as a food source. The embargo meant that the United States would no longer supply them with grain.

Carter also withdrew American athletes from the 1980 Olympic Games. This was among the most difficult things he had to do during his presidency. The Olympics were taking place in Moscow, the capital of the Soviet Union. The Soviets would earn a great deal of money by hosting the games. Carter did not want to support them in any way until

Carter signed the SALT II Treaty with Soviet leader Leonid Brezhnev. This agreement limited the number of nuclear weapons that both countries could develop. Congress still had to approve the agreement as well. But after the Soviets invaded Afghanistan, Carter asked Congress to delay its decision until the Soviets withdrew their troops.

they took their troops out of Afghanistan. Other nations agreed with Carter's decision. In fact, 62 other nations did not send teams to the Olympics that year.

Unfortunately, Carter's efforts had little positive effect. For one thing, the Soviets did not leave Afghanistan until 1988. Even worse, his actions had caused problems for Americans. The embargo hurt American farmers, who suffered because they sold fewer crops. American athletes who had trained all their lives for the Olympics lost their chance to compete in the 1980 games.

Probably the most troublesome issue Carter faced was the Iranian **Hostage** Crisis. In January of 1979, Iran's leader, Shah Mohammad Reza Pahlavi, had been **exiled** from his homeland. A religious leader, the Ayatollah Khomeini (pronounced eye-yah-TOL-uh koh-MAY-nee), took over the Iranian government. The Ayatollah did not like the United States. American relations with Iran suffered.

The United States had good relations with Iran while the shah (shown at right) was in power. But many Iranians felt that the shah was not a good leader. He liked the way of life in Western countries, such as the United States. Iranians worried he would change Iran forever, taking away its religious traditions and its culture. He was accused of illegal actions that hurt the people of his country.

29

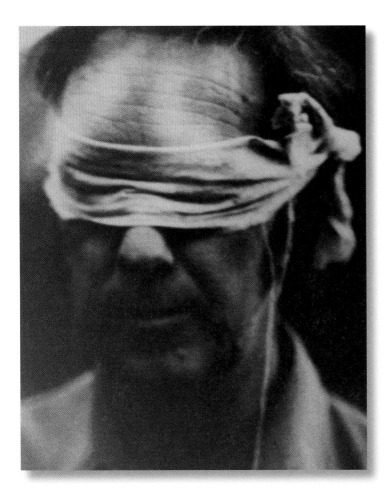

The Iranian terrorists issued this photograph of one of the hostages to newspapers around the world. Americans worried about what would happen to the captives.

The shah traveled to the Bahamas and then to Mexico, looking for a home. Then he announced he had cancer and wanted to come to America for treatment. But Carter worried that this would ruin America's already troubled relationship with Iran. He also knew the shah had not always cared about the human rights of Iran's citizens.

Finally, Carter allowed the shah to come to the United States. In protest, a mob of Iranian students seized the American Embassy in the Iranian capital of Tehran. On November 4, they captured 66 American hostages. They demanded that the United States return the shah to Iran.

The hostage crisis lasted for more than a year. It took up most of President Carter's time. He worried constantly about the American hostages.

THE CAMP DAVID ACCORDS LED to an important treaty between Egypt and Israel that ended conflict between the two nations. Prime Minister Begin, President Carter, and President Sadat signed the treaty at the White House on March 26, 1979.

When countries sign a treaty, both sides promise to abide by certain agreements. Israel and Egypt agreed to a number of things. First, Israel promised to return Egypt's land on the Sinai Peninsula. It also promised to remove its military forces there. The Egyptians agreed to let the Israelis use its important waterway, the Suez Canal. They also agreed to sell oil from Sinai to the Israelis. Finally, the Israelis promised to begin peace negotiations with other Arabs in the Middle East. They agreed to negotiations that would give the Palestinians more rights in the region, including the right to set up their own government.

A few days after they signed the treaty, Begin and Sadat met again in Cairo. They agreed to set up a special telephone hotline so they could easily contact each other. Israel also planned to return part of Sinai to Egypt ahead of schedule. It seemed that the treaty had truly accomplished something. Perhaps peace in the Middle East was possible.

Not everyone approved of the treaty. Other Arab leaders still believed that Israel had no right to lands in the Middle East. Even some Egyptians believed Sadat had given Israel more than it deserved. His enemies wanted to stop him from making further agreements with the Israelis. Sadat was **assassinated** on October 6, 1981. Unfortunately, the Middle East still struggles for peace.

Chapter FOUR

After the Presidency

Carter spent much of his last year as president trying to free the hostages. He hoped to find a peaceful way to end the crisis, but the terrorists refused to make an agreement.

THE HOSTAGE CRISIS MADE THE LAST YEAR OF Carter's presidency a difficult one. In the spring of 1980, he approved a plan to rescue the hostages. On April 24, a secret helicopter mission, called "Operation Eagle Claw," was sent to Iran.

First, a group of eight helicopters was to fly to Desert One, a location about 70 miles south of Tehran. From there, the operation would fly to the hills east of Tehran. Unfortunately, disaster struck at Desert One. Only five helicopters made it there. The other three were forced to land because of a dust storm. A minimum of six helicopters was necessary for a successful mission. The plan had to be canceled. But as one of the helicopters was leaving Desert One, its propellers kicked up

After the failed mission to save the hostages, one American helicopter lay in ruins.

a huge cloud of dust. The pilot couldn't see through the dust cloud, and the helicopter smashed into a small airplane. Eight Americans died in the accident.

The failed rescue mission only made things worse between the United States and Iran. Following the rescue attempt, the terrorists hid the hostages throughout the country. The shah died in July, but this made no difference. Americans began to think Carter had seriously mishandled the situation. The next election was coming up in November, and the hostage crisis hurt his chance of winning. On Election Day, Ronald Reagan easily defeated Carter and became the nation's 40th president.

33

Americans who had been held hostage in Iran were welcomed home with a ceremony at the White House when they returned to the United States.

That same month, Iran sent a message to the United States. It had a list of conditions for the hostages' release. An agreement was finally announced on January 19, 1981, the day before Reagan's inauguration.

It wasn't until after Carter left office that the hostages were actually released. On January 20, the day of President Reagan's inauguration, word reached Americans that the hostages were on their way home. Carter worked on negotiations until the moment President Reagan took office. Unfortunately, many Americans gave the new president credit for solving the crisis.

On January 21, President Reagan sent Carter to meet the hostages at a U.S. military base in Germany. It was an emotional homecoming for everybody involved—especially the former president who had struggled so hard to win their freedom.

Carter's strong commitment to human rights did not end after his presidency. It would guide him in all future activities. The Carters soon began to devote most of their time to helping people all over the world.

In 1982, Carter became a professor at Emory University in Atlanta, Georgia. He enjoyed his work at the university, but he wanted to do more to help people. He realized that people in countries all over the world lived in difficult, life-threatening situations caused by war, disease, **famine,** and poverty. He believed he could find ways to help.

In 1986, Jimmy and Rosalynn Carter founded the Carter Center. This organization has an important mission—to end human suffering. The goals of the Carter Center are to "prevent and resolve conflicts, enhance freedom and democracy, and improve health." Its vision is that everybody in the world should be able to live in peace.

Several different teams work at the center. Some teams focus on helping nations build democracies. The center has helped run elections in more than 20 countries, including Venezuela, Mexico, and Peru. By doing so, it has given people the freedom to vote for democratic leaders and take part in their governments. Representatives from the Carter

Many nations around the world do not allow their citizens to choose their own leaders. Representatives from the Carter Center have helped nations run democratic elections. Jimmy and Rosalynn Carter are shown here observing the 1999 election in Indonesia.

Center also have negotiated peaceful solutions to problems in countries such as Sudan, Bosnia, and Korea.

Some workers from the Carter Center fight disease. Others teach farmers how to grow more food for their families. Rosalynn Carter heads the center's program to aid Americans with mental illness.

One of the Carter Center's biggest programs is The Atlanta Project. It works to help people in Atlanta's most troubled neighborhoods. Health clinics and preschools have been built in these neighborhoods. The center also has after-school programs to give young people a safe place to go.

In addition to his work at the center, Carter has written many books. He writes about topics that are important to him. He wrote a book on the history of the Middle East called *Blood of Abraham* (1985). He also wrote a book about negotiation called *Negotiation: The Alternative to Hostility* (1984). And he wrote a book about the environment called *An Outdoor Journal* (1988).

Finally, Jimmy and Rosalynn Carter devote their energy to Habitat for Humanity. This organization builds houses for low-income families in countries all around the world. Without Habitat for Humanity, these families could not afford to buy their own homes.

As Jimmy left the White House in January of 1981, he promised himself that he would continue to be a world leader. He spoke the following words that would chart the course of the rest of his life:

"The battle for human rights—at home and abroad—is far from over. We should never be surprised or discouraged because the impact of our efforts has had, and will always have, varied results. Rather, we should take pride that the ideals that gave birth to our nation still inspire the hopes of people around the world."

1924 James Earl "Jimmy" Carter is born on October 1 in Plains, Georgia.

1941 Carter graduates from Plains High School. He enrolls at Georgia Southwestern College in Americus, Georgia, that fall.

1942 Carter transfers to the Georgia Institute of Technology.

1943 Carter is accepted to the U.S. Naval Academy in Annapolis, Maryland.

1946 Carter graduates from the Naval Academy. On July 7, he marries Rosalynn Smith.

1953 After his father dies, Carter leaves the U.S. Navy after seven years of service to return to Plains. There he runs the family business and peanut farm.

1962 Carter is elected to the Georgia State Senate.

1966 Carter runs for governor of Georgia but loses the election.

1970 Carter is elected governor of Georgia. He holds the post until 1975. By 1972, he is already thinking about running for president.

1976 The Democratic Party nominates Carter as its presidential candidate. He runs against President Gerald Ford. Carter wins in a close election.

1977 Carter is inaugurated the 39th president of the United States on January 20. He establishes the Department of Energy on August 4. Carter and Panama leader General Omar Torrijos Herrera sign the Panama Canal treaty on September 7.

1978 The Camp David Summit begins on September 4. Carter hopes to help negotiate a peace treaty between Israel's Prime Minister Begin and Egypt's President Sadat. After 13 days of meetings, the Camp David Accords are created.

1979 The shah of Iran is exiled from his country in January. By February 1, the Ayatollah Khomeini has taken over the Iranian government. On March 26, Begin, Carter, and Sadat sign the Egyptian-Israeli peace treaty. Soviet leader Leonid Breshnev and President Carter sign the SALT II Treaty on June 18. The Department of Education is formed on October 17. Terrorists take over the American Embassy in Tehran on November 4. They take Americans hostage. The Soviet Union invades Afghanistan on December 27.

1980 Carter boycotts the 1980 Olympic Games, which are held in Moscow, the capital of the Soviet Union. He does this to protest the Soviet invasion of Afghanistan. Carter and his advisors decide to attempt a hostage rescue mission. On April 24, the rescue mission, "Operation Eagle Claw," begins. The attempt fails, and eight Americans are killed. Republicans nominate Ronald Reagan as their presidential candidate in July. Reagan defeats Carter on Election Day. Carter signs the Alaska Lands Bill in December.

1981 The final terms for the release of the American hostages in Iran are negotiated during Carter's final days as president. Ronald Reagan is inaugurated president on January 20 at noon. Twenty minutes later, the hostages are released in Tehran. The next day, President Reagan sends Carter to a U.S. military base in Germany to welcome the hostages home.

1982 Carter becomes a professor at Emory University in Atlanta, Georgia.

1986 Jimmy and Rosalynn Carter found the Carter Center.

1991 Carter announces The Atlanta Project.

1999 Rosalynn and Jimmy Carter receive the Presidential Medal of Freedom in August. On December 14, Carter travels to Central America to prepare for the transfer of control of the Panama Canal. On December 31, a ceremony is held to turn the canal over to Panama.

assassinate (uh-SASS-uh-nayt)
Assassinate means to murder someone, especially a well-known person. Anwar Sadat was assassinated in 1981.

bill (BILL)
A bill is an idea for a new law that is presented to a group of lawmakers. Carter introduced a bill to help solve the energy crisis of the 1970s.

candidate (KAN-duh-det)
A candidate is a person running in an election. Carter was the Democratic candidate for president in 1976 and 1980.

communism (KOM-yeh-niz-em)
Communism is a system of govern-ment in which the central government, not the people, hold all the power. Americans worried the Soviet Union wanted to spread communism to other countries in 1979.

conserve (kun-SERV)
If people conserve energy, they save or do not waste it. Carter urged Americans to conserve energy in the 1970s.

deforestation (dee-for-es-TAY-shun)
Deforestation is the process of cutting down forests, either for wood products or to use the land. Deforestation threatens wilderness areas.

democracy (deh-MAW-kruh-see)
A democracy is a country in which the government is run by the people who live there. The United States is a democracy.

embargo (em-BAR-goh)
An embargo is when one country stops selling a product to another country to make it agree to do something. During the grain embargo of 1980, the United States sold no grain to the Soviet Union.

engineering (en-jeh-NEER-ing)
Engineering is the science of building engines, machines, roads, and other things. Carter studied engineering at the U.S. Naval Academy.

exile (EG-zyl)
If people are exiled from their country, they are forced to leave. The shah of Iran was exiled from his country in 1979.

famine (FAM-en)
Famine is a serious lack of food that causes people to starve. The Carter Center fights famine.

hostage (HOS-tij)
A hostage is a person held prisoner until some demand is agreed to. The American hostages were held by terrorists in Iran for 444 days.

inauguration (ih-nawg-yuh-RAY-shun)
An inauguration is the ceremony that takes place when a new president begins a term. Carter's presidential inauguration took place in January of 1977.

inflation (in-FLAY-shun)
Inflation is a sharp and sudden rise in the price of goods. Inflation had been a problem for many years when Carter became president.

negotiate (neh-GO-she-ayt)
If people negotiate, they talk things over and try to come to an agreement. Carter helped negotiate a treaty between Egypt and Israel.

politicians (pawl-ih-TISH-unz)
A politician is a person who holds an office in government. As a young boy, Carter listened to politicians speak at barbecues.

scandal (SKAN-dl)
A scandal is a shameful action that shocks the public. The Watergate scandal made Americans distrust the nation's leaders.

segregation (seg-rih-GAY-shun)
In the southern United States, segregation was the practice of keeping black people and white people separated. Carter's mother taught him that segregation was wrong.

Soviet Union (SOH-vee-et YOON-yen)
The Soviet Union was a communist country that stretched from eastern Europe across Asia to the Pacific Ocean. It separated into several smaller countries in 1991.

summit (SUM-it)
A summit is a meeting of important government officials. The leaders of Egypt, Israel, and the United States met at the Camp David Summit in 1978.

treaty (TREE-tee)
A treaty is a formal agreement between nations. Carter negotiated many treaties with other nations.

President	Birthplace	Life Span	Presidency	Political Party	First Lady
George Washington	Virginia	1732–1799	1789–1797	None	Martha Dandridge Custis Washington
John Adams	Massachusetts	1735–1826	1797–1801	Federalist	Abigail Smith Adams
Thomas Jefferson	Virginia	1743–1826	1801–1809	Democratic-Republican	widower
James Madison	Virginia	1751–1836	1809–1817	Democratic Republican	Dolley Payne Todd Madison
James Monroe	Virginia	1758–1831	1817–1825	Democratic Republican	Elizabeth Kortright Monroe
John Quincy Adams	Massachusetts	1767–1848	1825–1829	Democratic-Republican	Louisa Johnson Adams
Andrew Jackson	South Carolina	1767–1845	1829–1837	Democrat	widower
Martin Van Buren	New York	1782–1862	1837–1841	Democrat	widower
William H. Harrison	Virginia	1773–1841	1841	Whig	Anna Symmes Harrison
John Tyler	Virginia	1790–1862	1841–1845	Whig	Letitia Christian Tyler Julia Gardiner Tyler
James K. Polk	North Carolina	1795–1849	1845–1849	Democrat	Sarah Childress Polk

Our PRESIDENTS

President	Birthplace	Life Span	Presidency	Political Party	First Lady
Zachary Taylor	Virginia	1784–1850	1849–1850	Whig	Margaret Mackall Smith Taylor
Millard Fillmore	New York	1800–1874	1850–1853	Whig	Abigail Powers Fillmore
Franklin Pierce	New Hampshire	1804–1869	1853–1857	Democrat	Jane Means Appleton Pierce
James Buchanan	Pennsylvania	1791–1868	1857–1861	Democrat	never married
Abraham Lincoln	Kentucky	1809–1865	1861–1865	Republican	Mary Todd Lincoln
Andrew Johnson	North Carolina	1808–1875	1865–1869	Democrat	Eliza McCardle Johnson
Ulysses S. Grant	Ohio	1822–1885	1869–1877	Republican	Julia Dent Grant
Rutherford B. Hayes	Ohio	1822–1893	1877–1881	Republican	Lucy Webb Hayes
James A. Garfield	Ohio	1831–1881	1881	Republican	Lucretia Rudolph Garfield
Chester A. Arthur	Vermont	1829–1886	1881–1885	Republican	widower
Grover Cleveland	New Jersey	1837–1908	1885–1889	Democrat	Frances Folsom Cleveland

President	Birthplace	Life Span	Presidency	Political Party	First Lady
Benjamin Harrison	Ohio	1833–1901	1889–1893	Republican	Caroline Scott Harrison
Grover Cleveland	New Jersey	1837–1908	1893–1897	Democrat	Frances Folsom Cleveland
William McKinley	Ohio	1843–1901	1897–1901	Republican	Ida Saxton McKinley
Theodore Roosevelt	New York	1858–1919	1901–1909	Republican	Edith Kermit Carow Roosevelt
William H. Taft	Ohio	1857–1930	1909–1913	Republican	Helen Herron Taft
Woodrow Wilson	Virginia	1856–1924	1913–1921	Democrat	Ellen L. Axson Wilson Edith Bolling Galt Wilson
Warren G. Harding	Ohio	1865–1923	1921–1923	Republican	Florence Kling De Wolfe Harding
Calvin Coolidge	Vermont	1872–1933	1923–1929	Republican	Grace Goodhue Coolidge
Herbert C. Hoover	Iowa	1874–1964	1929–1933	Republican	Lou Henry Hoover
Franklin D. Roosevelt	New York	1882–1945	1933–1945	Democrat	Anna Eleanor Roosevelt Roosevelt
Harry S. Truman	Missouri	1884–1972	1945–1953	Democrat	Elizabeth Wallace Truman

Our PRESIDENTS

President	Birthplace	Life Span	Presidency	Political Party	First Lady
Dwight D. Eisenhower	Texas	1890–1969	1953–1961	Republican	Mary "Mamie" Doud Eisenhower
John F. Kennedy	Massachusetts	1917–1963	1961–1963	Democrat	Jacqueline Bouvier Kennedy
Lyndon B. Johnson	Texas	1908–1973	1963–1969	Democrat	Claudia Alta Taylor Johnson
Richard M. Nixon	California	1913–1994	1969–1974	Republican	Thelma Catherine Ryan Nixon
Gerald Ford	Nebraska	1913–	1974–1977	Republican	Elizabeth "Betty" Bloomer Warren Ford
James Carter	Georgia	1924–	1977–1981	Democrat	Rosalynn Smith Carter
Ronald Reagan	Illinois	1911–	1981–1989	Republican	Nancy Davis Reagan
George Bush	Massachusetts	1924–	1989–1993	Republican	Barbara Pierce Bush
 William Clinton	Arkansas	1946–	1993–2001	Democrat	Hillary Rodham Clinton
George W. Bush	Connecticut	1946–	2001–	Republican	Laura Welch Bush

Presidential FACTS

Qualifications
To run for president, a candidate must
- be at least 35 years old
- be a citizen who was born in the United States
- have lived in the United States for 14 years

Term of Office
A president's term of office is four years. No president can stay in office for more than two terms.

Election Date
The presidential election takes place every four years on the first Tuesday of November.

Inauguration Date
Presidents are inaugurated on January 20.

Oath of Office
I do solemnly swear I will faithfully execute the office of the President of the United States and will to the best of my ability preserve, protect, and defend the Constitution of the United States.

Write a Letter to the President
One of the best things about being a U.S. citizen is that Americans get to participate in their government. They can speak out if they feel government leaders aren't doing their jobs. They can also praise leaders who are going the extra mile. Do you have something you'd like the president to do? Should the president worry more about the environment and encourage people to recycle? Should the government spend more money on our schools? You can write a letter to the president to say how you feel!

1600 Pennsylvania Avenue
Washington, D.C. 20500

You can even send an e-mail to: president@whitehouse.gov

For Further INFORMATION

Internet Sites

Visit the Carter Presidential Library:
http://carterlibrary.galileo.peachnet.edu/

Visit the Carter Center:
http://www.cartercenter.org

Learn more about the Panama Canal:
http://www.pancanal.com/

Learn more about Habitat for Humanity:
http://www.habitat.org/

Learn more about all the presidents and visit the White House:
http://www.whitehouse.gov/WH/glimpse/presidents/html/presidents.html
http://www.thepresidency.org/presinfo.htm
http://www.americanpresidents.org/

Books

Altman, Linda Jacobs. *The Creation of Israel.* San Diego, CA: Lucent Books, 1998.

Carter, J. *Talking Peace: A Vision for the Next Generation.* New York: Dutton Childrens Books, 1993.

George, Linda, and Charles George. *Jimmy Carter: Builder of Peace.* Chicago: Childrens Press, 2000.

Long, Cathryn J. *The Middle East in Search of Peace.* Brookfield, CT: Millbrook Press, 1993.

Sandak, R. Cass. *The Carters* (First Families). New York: Crestwood House, 1993.

Stein, R. Conrad. *The Iran Hostage Crisis.* Chicago: Childrens Press, 1989.

Index